T0000314

THANK A FARMER

MARIA GIANFERRARI

Illustrated by
MONICA MIKAI

THANK A FARMER

Norton Young Readers
An Imprint of W. W. Norton & Company
Celebrating a Century of Independent Publishing

In memory of my beloved "Zia" Adriana Papani,
and thank you/grazie to all "I miei parenti contadini."

—M.G.

Dedicated to Mother Earth, every farmer, and the animal
and plant kingdoms. Together you nourish us all.

—M.M.

Text copyright © 2023 by Maria Gianferrari
Illustration copyright © 2023 by Monica Mikai

For information about permission to reproduce selections from this book,
write to Permissions, W. W. Norton & Company, Inc., 500 Fifth Avenue, New York, NY 10110

For information about special discounts for bulk purchases, please contact
W. W. Norton Special Sales at specialsales@wwnorton.com or 800-233-4830

Manufacturing by RRD Asia
Book design by Hana Anouk Nakamura
Production manager: Delaney Adams

ISBN 978-1-324-01579-6

W. W. Norton & Company, Inc.
500 Fifth Avenue, New York, N.Y. 10110
www.wwnorton.com

W. W. Norton & Company Ltd.
15 Carlisle Street, London W1D 3BS

1 2 3 4 5 6 7 8 9 0

If you like the food on your table,
THANK A FARMER.

If you like bread for breakfast,
THANK A FARMER.

Combine sweeps
Winter wheat—
Chop.
Kernels pop from chaff—
Plop
Into the hopper.
Rain into grain carts
and storage elevators
For milling
And grinding into flour.

Thank a farmer for your bread,
Fresh and hearty.

If you like your cereal with milk,
THANK A FARMER.

Dairy cows
Wear white-black-brown.
Milked by hand,
Squeeze.
Squirt.
Ping into the pail;
Or by machine
Milk flows
Through the hose
Ready for pick up.

Thank a dairy farmer for your milk,
Smooth and silky.

If you like your summer salad and a variety of vegetables,
THANK A FARMER.

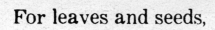
For leaves and seeds,

Stems and flowers,
Bulbs and tubers,

Fruits and roots.

Thank a farmer for your fruits
and veggies,
Nourishing and nutritious.

If there are berries and
cherries in your bowl,
THANK A FARMER.

Farm workers follow
The sun
And the seasons.
Berries bloom
On the vine,
Ripe for picking:
Pinch.
Pluck.
Pull.
Fill the punnet.

Machines help workers too:
Tree shakers
Clamp the trunk.
Upside-down-umbrella unfolds
Shake-shake-shake—
Fruit falls down,
Then up the belt,
And into the bin.
Fold in,
Begin again.

Thank a farm worker for your berries,
Sweet and tangy.

If you like peanut butter and jelly sandwiches,
THANK A FARMER!

Peanut pods
Grow underground.
Diggers pull up plants,
Shake off soil.
Plants lie upside-down to dry.
Pickers peel off pods,
Pop into the hopper.
Vines lie in the fields.
Peanuts dry and roast,
Grind into peanut butter.

Thank a farmer for your peanut butter,
Creamy and crunchy.

If you like rice for breakfast,
lunch, or dinner,
THANK A FARMER.

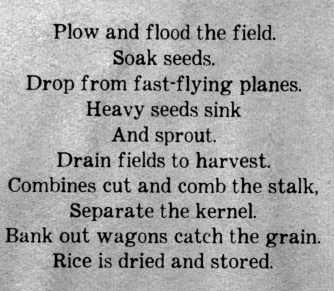

Plow and flood the field.
Soak seeds.
Drop from fast-flying planes.
Heavy seeds sink
And sprout.
Drain fields to harvest.
Combines cut and comb the stalk,
Separate the kernel.
Bank out wagons catch the grain.
Rice is dried and stored.

Thank a farmer for your wild rice too!
Harvested by hand,
Polers propel the boat.
Knockers bend the stalk
Over the hull.

Tap.
Grains plonk.
Dry in the sun.
Parch in a pot.
Thresh the chaff,
And winnow.

Thank farmers for all kinds
of rice,
Fluffy and filling.

If you like mushrooms on your pizza,
THANK A FARMER.

Mushrooms grow
In compost beds,
Stacked on shelves.
Add some spawn.
Place the peat moss.
Up
Pop
Mushrooms!
Push-twist-turn-trim.
Pack-sort-ship.
Recycle,
And begin again.

Thank a farmer for
your mushrooms,
Earthy and chewy.

If you like your sweaters and socks,
THANK A FARMER.

Spring is time for
Shearing fleece.
Buzz.
Slide.
Fleece glides
Off.
Wash.
Card.
Spin some yarn.

Thank a farmer for
your winter wool,
Warm and cozy.

Thank farmers in winter
For your maple syrup, too!

Drill a hole.
Tap the spile.
Hang the bucket.
Cold nights,
Warm days,
Sap flows
Through rubber veins.
Boiled until brown.
Smell
Cotton-candy
sweetness.

Thank a farmer for your maple syrup,
Sugary and sticky!

If you like your food fresh-picked,
THANK A FARMER.

For rooftop hives
And honeybees.
For hens
And hoop houses.
For hanging baskets full of fruits,
And vining vegetables.
For shelves streaming with lettuce.
For greens growing
Up:
Hydro-aero-aquaponics.

Garden in a city lot
Or schoolyard plot.
In planters
Boxes
And backyard pots!

Thank farmers everywhere for your fresh food,
And be one too!

Farmers are thankful
for their helpers:
People planting
And picking.
Animals carrying,
Growing,
Giving.
Machines plowing,
Planting,
Plucking,
And harvesting.

Farmers are thankful for—
Soil and sun.
Water and worms.
Birds and bats,
For butterflies,
Bees,
And even trees!

If you like the food on your table . . .

THANK YOU, FARMERS! This is a small survey of farming methods. There are many more types of farming than we have featured here.

WHEAT

Winter wheat is planted mid-August through October and is harvested mid-May through July. It's higher in protein and works well in pastas and breads. Winter wheat also helps prevent weed growth and *erosion*, the wearing-away of topsoil.

COWS

Dairy cows are milked two to three times a day. A cow produces seven gallons of milk—that's 400 glasses—in one day! There are many different breeds of dairy cows. One of the most common ones is the black-and-white Holstein. Milk is made into butter, yogurt, cheese, and ice cream. Goat, sheep, camel, and water buffalo milk is also used to create dairy products.

LETTUCE

Yuma, Arizona, the "winter lettuce capital of the world," supplies 90% of head, leaf, and romaine lettuce consumed in winter in the United States. Located in the Sonoran Desert, Yuma receives 350 days of sunshine a year and little rainfall, so farmers water their crops using irrigation, channeling water from the nearby Colorado River.

LEAVES & SEEDS; STEMS & FLOWERS; BULBS & TUBERS; FRUITS & ROOTS

Vegetables come in many forms. Some examples of leaves include brussels sprouts, spinach, watercress, and bok choy. Seed vegetables like green beans, peas, edamame, and sweet corn grow in pods. Stems are the edible stalks of plants, like celery and asparagus, while flowers include broccoli, cauliflower, and artichokes. Fennel, garlic, leeks, and onions grow just below the ground as bulbs, and tubers such as potatoes and yams grow a bit deeper. Fruits contain seeds: tomatoes, squashes, and melons. Root vegetables include carrots, turnips, beets, and radishes. Many tomatoes, peppers, and other fruits are grown inside, in giant greenhouses.

BERRIES & CHERRIES

Many berries are still harvested by hand by seasonal farm workers. Some farmers use machine harvesters with upside-down U-shaped holes that drive over the berry bushes to collect berries. Cherries can be either hand- or machine-harvested by a hydraulic tree shaker. California is the top strawberry producer. Washington State grows the majority of sweet cherries, while most tart cherries come from Wisconsin.

PEANUTS

Georgia's top crop is the peanut, which is technically a legume (member of the pea family). Unlike most plants, peanuts flower above ground but fruit below ground. Scientist and inventor Dr. George Washington Carver created more than 300 different products from peanuts, ranging from foods such as cooking oil and instant coffee to toiletries like soaps, shampoos, and lotions as well as products like paper, ink, and gasoline.

RICE

Rice grows in fields called *checks*. It is sown using airplanes in California; it's also grown in the "rice belt" states of Texas, Louisiana, Mississippi, Arkansas, and Missouri. Rice grows best in clay soil, which retains water. Flooding reduces weed growth and repels insects.

Wild rice: Wild rice is the seed of an aquatic grass that grows naturally in the muddy soil of watersheds in the Great Lakes region. Ripened grains fall off the stalks into the water, sprout in spring, and fruit in late summer. Wild rice is hand-harvested with sticks called *knockers*. To the Anishinaabeg people, wild rice is *manoomin*, a sacred food and medicine used in ceremonies, in traditional stories and celebrations, in mourning, and to recover from sickness. Wild rice has been a part of their spiritual and cultural identity for many centuries, and continues to be so today.

The Red Lake Nation in Minnesota sells traditional hand-harvested rice and grows paddy and cultivated seed rice for commercial use. The White Earth Nation, also in Minnesota, is home to the most wild rice beds—nearly 50 lakes and more than 500 other bodies of water. On a good day, hundreds of pounds of wild rice can be collected.

MUSHROOMS

Mushrooms are the fruit of fungi and grow from spores, not seeds. They don't require light in order to grow, only moisture and moderate temperatures. Some mushrooms grow in a substrate (surface) of straw, hay, manure, gypsum (a mineral), and moss; others grow best on wood. The substrate is *pasteurized*, or heated up, to kill unwanted microorganisms. Mushrooms can double in size in 24 hours! Fifty percent of the United States' mushrooms come from Chester County, Pennsylvania. Button mushrooms are the most common ones. Never eat a mushroom that you find outdoors—many are highly poisonous.

FIBER

Wool comes from the shorn fleece of sheep and is woven into yarn and cloth. Lambswool, as its name suggests, comes from lambs under seven months old. Originating in Spain, Merino wool comes from Merino sheep. Wool also comes from goats, rabbits, alpacas, and llamas. Animal fleece is shorn by shearers in late spring or early summer. The top wool-producing U.S. states include Wyoming, Colorado, and Utah, along with Texas and California.

MAPLE SYRUP

Indigenous and First Nations peoples have been tapping sugar maple trees for many generations for the medicinal and preservative properties of their sap, and to make maple sugars and syrup. Colonizers in Canada, New England, and the Great Lakes regions copied this process of collecting maple sap to produce maple syrup commercially. It takes approximately 40 gallons of sap to make 1 gallon of syrup.

URBAN & VERTICAL FARMING

Urban and vertical farming can help make fresh-picked produce available in urban areas known as food deserts, where there are few grocery stores or farmers' markets available for residents. Fruits and vegetables grown indoors on shelves can be freshly harvested and delivered locally. City chickens provide fresh eggs, and bees produce fresh honey. Local residents and restaurants can help farmers by collecting food scraps, coffee grounds, and tea leaves for compost to make healthy soil with the help of red wiggler worms.

FARMERS ARE THANKFUL FOR . . .

Soil: Soil is a vital natural resource. Healthy soil regulates water and sustains plant and animal life; its minerals and microbes filter out pollutants. Soil stores and transforms nutrients like carbon, nitrogen, and phosphorus that help plants grow. It also stabilizes plant roots, preventing erosion. Adding animal waste (or *manure*) to soil increases carbon and phosphorus levels, raises organic-matter content, and improves structure and water retention.

Worms: Worms are decomposers; they help to break down food and other materials into nutrient-rich soils through their *castings*, or poop, a process known as *vermicomposting*. Red wiggler worms are ideal for composting because they don't burrow deeply.

Pollinators: Wasps and moths, as well as bees, butterflies, and birds—especially hummingbirds—help to pollinate plants when they feed on nectar. In warmer regions, mammals like *nectorivorous* (nectar-eating) bats also help to pollinate plants.

Pest management: Bats and birds practice pest control. They help to save crops by eating all manner of insects and their larvae. Insect infestations can weaken a plant's defenses, and this stress makes plants more susceptible to harmful fungi.

Trees: The practice of *agroforestry*, combining the planting of trees and crops, creates healthy soil with the help of *mycorrhizal* fungi (fungi that grow on tree and plant roots) and windbreaks, both of which prevent soil erosion. It also creates wildlife habitats.

FURTHER READING

Before We Eat: From Farm to Table by Pat Brisson, illustrated by Mary Azarian (Tilbury House Publishers, 2018)

Compost Stew: An A to Z Recipe for the Earth by Mary McKenna Siddals, illustrated by Ashley Wolff (Dragonfly Books, 2014)

Farmer Will Allen and the Growing Table by Jacqueline Briggs Martin, illustrated by Eric Shabazz Larkin (Readers to Eaters, 2016)

Farming by Gail Gibbons (Holiday House, 2019)

The Farm That Feeds Us: A Year in the Life of an Organic Farm by Nancy Castaldo, illustrated by Ginnie Hsu (Words & Pictures, 2020)

Honeybee: The Busy Life of Apis Mellifera by Candace Fleming, illustrated by Eric Rohmann (Neal Porter Books, 2020)

How Did That Get in My Lunchbox? The Story of Food by Chris Butterworth, illustrated by Lucia Gaggiotti (Candlewick Press, 2013)

I Am Farmer: Growing an Environmental Movement in Cameroon by Baptiste & Miranda Paul, illustrated by Elizabeth Zunon (Millbrook Press, 2019)

Right This Very Minute: A Table-to-Farm Book About Food and Farming by Lisl H. Detlefsen, illustrated by Renée Kurilla (Feeding Minds Press, 2019)

Thank You, Garden by Liz Garton Scanlon, illustrated by Simone Shin (Beach Lane Books, 2020)

Up in the Garden and Down in the Dirt by Kate Messner, illustrated by Christopher Silas Neal (Chronicle Books, 2015)

The Vegetables We Eat by Gail Gibbons (Holiday House, 2008)

Who Made My Lunch? series by Bridget Heos, illustrated by Stephanie Fizer Coleman (Amicus Ink)

FURTHER VIEWING

American's Heartland (2005–present). A PBS series celebrating farmers in all 50 states: https://www.americasheartland.org

The Biggest Little Farm (2018). Follow documentary-maker John Chester and his wife, Molly, a chef, as they establish a sustainable farm outside of Los Angeles, California: https://www.biggestlittlefarmmovie.com

FarmHer. Sharing stories of women farmers: https://farmher.com/farmher-on-rfd-tv/

Virtual Farm Trips. https://virtualfarmtrips.com

WEBSITES

4H STEM and Agriculture Program: https://4-h.org/parents/stem-agriculture/

Ben & Jerry: How We Make Ice Cream: https://www.benjerry.com/flavors/how-we-make-ice-cream

My American Farm: Fun Farm Games for Cool Kids: http://www.myamericanfarm.org

National Agriculture in the Classroom: https://agclassroom.org//

National FFA Organization (formerly known as Future Farmers of America): https://www.ffa.org/about/